Bad Fame

BAD FAME

POEMS BY
Martin McGovern

ABLE MUSE PRESS

Copyright ©2015 by Martin McGovern
First published in 2015 by

Able Muse Press

www.ablemusepress.com

All rights reserved. No part of this book may be used or reproduced in any manner whatsoever without written permission except in the case of brief quotations embedded in critical articles and reviews. Requests for permission should be addressed to the Able Muse Press editor at editor@ablemuse.com

Printed in the United States of America

Library of Congress Control Number: 2015931122

ISBN 978-1-927409-50-3 (paperback)
ISBN 978-1-927409-51-0 (digital)

Cover image: "Through a Window" by Joslyn Winters

Cover & book design by Alexander Pepple

Able Muse Press is an imprint of *Able Muse*: A Review of Poetry, Prose & Art—at www.ablemuse.com

Able Muse Press
467 Saratoga Avenue #602
San Jose, CA 95129

For Gabriel Synge Crain McGovern—

the most beautiful gift of all

Acknowledgments

I am grateful to the editors of the following journals where many of these poems originally appeared, sometimes in earlier versions.

Denver Quarterly: "For Delia."
The Gettysburg Review: "If the Light Could Kill Us."
Hotel Amerika: "Socrates and the Locusts," "Those Years."
In Art: "The Circle of Late Afternoon."
The New Republic: "The Rainbow Diary."
Poetry: "All Hallows Eve / Anniversary," "Christmas, Colorado," "For Charles and Mary Lamb," "Processionalia," "Summer Indians," "Toward an Epithalamion."
Shenandoah: "Chanteuse with Dog, Walking."
Western Humanities Review: "Tonight the Lace Curtain."

I would like to thank the following people for their love and their support of my art and life: David Lazar, Kendra Crain, Dermod Downs, James and Kate Gale, the Gauthiers, Britta Erickson, Steven Deidel, Steve Barbour, Christopher Dyer, Laura Cowperthwaite, Carol Simpson, Rebekah Buric, Kevin Hastings, Charles Fontaine, Denis Davis, Sarah Smith, Tanya Lundstroth, John and Darlene McGovern, John Berry, Tim and Barbara, Marsha Recknagel, Barbara Sorensen, Jim Cannon, Gail and Porter Storey, Jeffrey Greene, and Kathryn Winograd.

Foreword

Poems as Train Rooms

MARTIN MCGOVERN LIVES SOMEWHERE between Graham Greene and the rectory, variable distances. Of course, that was also true of Graham Greene. But what makes this wayfaring space so recognizable, what lets us know that someone is home, is McGovern's radically brooding voice of philosophical uncertainty married to the warm heart of someone who feels unconscionably blessed. The married set of questions in McGovern's work are: how can I be (how can I not be) at peace in a landscape so marred with horrifying events, and in such a paradise as this, am I what is wrong with the picture? The two questions, or sets of questions, are sometimes overlapping. But in any case, the point is that there is an unforsaken paradise in these pages, and a lot of ungodly anxiety.

In "For Marian, a Mother," McGovern tells us that he "can't even dance," but asks, "So how did I end up leading such a charmed life?" We understand that he's fast on his feet ("Put down that ... broom— you're sweeping me off my feet"), and slow to accept the rewards. In "I Am Holding a Duckling I Won at the Fair," the confusion of rabbits and ducks, death and delivery, innocence and madness, is balanced into a kind of tonal nightmare; nothing might have more weight than anything else, and since we're subjects of the "coin toss" and "optical illusions" we may as well focus on the "mounds . . . of green mint" and not the "ashpit."

★

THIS WORLD can be just really very terrible but in a brilliantly surprising kind of way ("the alyssum/ and verbena bushes, ablaze with bees"). Alas, unredeemed. But sparkly and unpredictable. Our narrator has a childlike innocence. He asks questions that seem young—"you know what?"—until we realize that he's imagining looking out the window of a toy train in the family train room that houses the entire train set with its landscape of tiny trees and parks, people and towns. And what McGovern is seeing could stop you cold: someone slitting their leg, or slipping away. He's shocked, even astonished that memory, the images passing by in a room on a train, could be so blunt, so *blue,* and could so resemble the actual images that he has seen on buses or in the mountains.

Like *Dubliners, Bad Fame* darkens, deepens, darkens through its sections, understanding with Joyce the tidal pull of place that will never let us survive if we resist the current. So the "blue snow," not of Dublin, but of memory, of Colorado, of a family dressed for church, and a family underwater overtakes us. But we're touched by a host of saving graces—this voice, with its deep vein of comedy in the midst of despair, this extraordinarily unique McGovern flair for the Keatonish (Buster) aside mixed with lyrical intellection, these poetic rooms with their many blue lights, direct or indirect, for us to turn on as night comes on.

—David Lazar

Contents

Acknowledgments	*vi*
Foreword	*vii*

★

Today	*3*
For Marian, a Mother	*4*
The Circle of Late Afternoon	*5*
For Delia	*7*
Tonight the Lace Curtain	*9*
Socrates and the Locusts	*10*
If the Light Could Kill Us	*13*
Toward an Epithalamion	*14*

★

I Am Holding a Duckling I Won at the Fair	*19*
If Someone Gave Me an Earring	*20*
I Feel Guilty Watching You Sleep	*21*
I Can't Predict What I Think, I Said	*22*
Shim Sat and Shat on the Blue Tile Floor	*23*

★

Those Years	*27*
Hospital Corner	*29*
On the Welsh Coast: Homage to James Joyce	*31*
For Charles and Mary Lamb	*33*

★

Tonight Mars Is over by the Moon, Look	*43*
There, That's It	*44*
Chanteuse with Dog, Walking	*45*
Three for One	*46*
Contrecoup	*48*
This Is the Library Straight down from the Train Room	*49*

★

Processionalia	*53*
The Rainbow Diary	*55*
Christmas, Colorado	*56*
All Hallows Eve / Anniversary	*58*
Summer Indians	*61*

★

Blue	*67*

Bad Fame

"This is [not] the sorrowful state of souls unsure,
Whose lives earned neither honor nor bad fame. . . ."
  – Dante Alighieri, *The Inferno,* Canto III, tr. Robert Pinsky

Remember the words of the Lord Jesus, how he said, It is more blessed to give than to receive.
  – The Apostle Paul, *King James Bible,* Acts 20:35

Do you need anybody?
  – John Lennon and Paul McCartney,
    "With a Little Help from My Friends"

Today

The air is unhinged, I believe, and full of jazz.
Today, the red and yellow and gold trees told me to consider
this (for once): when you do something bad—
and, of course, who's to judge?—you insult all of humanity.
And who *is* to judge? Well, they are all right here,
all my brothers and sisters, right before my face.
How do you not weep for those who have died
innocently? How do you not "continue on," as they say?
How do we take care of each other? I don't even know you.
I do, though, want to take care of you. I don't know how.
You are my flesh—my brother, my sister—yes, you are
my flesh. I want to see you tomorrow and to bless you
and to bless you again and again and again. Always alive.

For Marian, a Mother

Maybe the power or the glory or the blue-handled oar or the shovel.
Whatever I dig up is mine or yours, I might be sorry to hear—
I can't even dance with myself, much less anyone else.
What will the preachers say about that, what all the fair mothers?
The latter, I am sure, will celebrate all the stars in the trees, all the
    whooshing of traffics.
When I take a deep breath, I see circles of amber, hear waters parting—
    they are so grand to swim in!
So how did I end up leading such a charmed life?
The flags on the masts, our mothers, are raising a terror—
they are at the same time laughing and crying and cheering us on.

The Circle of Late Afternoon

Trying to break the circle of late afternoon,
whatever I show of myself winds
outside myself
as truculently as the dirt road
outside Greeley, Colorado, curls through wheat fields
and goes nowhere.
So I drive until fatigued
before I can return
home where I want to be, where I do not,
where it is quiet and there is nothing
but a mirror over a foldout bed
and the porcelain statue of some dark saint
left on the windowsill by the tenant before me.

So I finally find comfort in the sound
of the rooster scratching gravel
outside my one window.
How forthright do I really want to be?
Isn't there an art to giving myself away slowly like wheat
opening to the sun, an art to the love I say
I give quietly?

Isn't there, where I drive, a small pond near a hill?
I turn on the radio, and person after person is reading an ad
    for someone to love.
The widower smokes a pipe and has three children.
He gets up early and will buy a new wife a car.

I decide I'll always move slowly
toward intimacy, as if in water,
as if the air, heavy from the stockyards, allowed me to reach
others only gradually. When it begins to rain,
I will go home. When I arrive,
I'll close the curtains, my eyes.
The gregarious saint will welcome me
and reassure me sometime
soon I will love all I know to their faces.

For Delia

Whatever quickens covers,
can cover, a slower
rhythm—the contrapuntal slough
and drive of spring muds
in southern Colorado:
we should have known the Huerfano
River's hachures disguised
suckholes, strong-willed
and impossible to deny. Dropping
to your knees three feet from
the limestone bank, you looked
like you were praying,
arms outstretched, blond
hair spreading on the water
like a gown. Arms locked
by my arms, it took ten full minutes
to torque your blond body out,
our fear a kind of music,
a sudden, stunning, stunned
rise of blood. We must
have looked pastoral, erotic,
afterward, to anyone watching
from a distance—like something,
something from Delius, Delia, both of us
sixteen, naked by the fire,
drying each other with a blanket.
If fear is a god, we were its

mystics, crouching and dusk-lit,
the slight paralysis it
stung your body's right side with,
clamping down your new mask—
primitive, delirious, half your face
a laugh and half a grimace.

Tonight the Lace Curtain

Shall we forget how much anything has meant,
since the noblest of deeds is falling away
with a doe-like coloring? Without you
the foyer would be only a facsimile,
risqué with suggestion, the sole ticking
of the hall clock. Your silhouette is sewn
into the lace curtain, and everyone else
has given way to you one more time.
Can you say goodbye without the fiercest
of jealousies? Can I say goodbye to you
without the fiercest of jealousies?
Last night the fan stopped like a bad heart.
Risk everything, I told myself. Risk
everything, you said aloud. The fan started,
sui generis, like a dog's affection.
Knickknacks on the credenza began telling
their tales: Could the Swiss elf play his sax
any more sweetly? Could the crystal ball
be any clearer about true joy and sorrow?
They had recorded our courtship—my zeal to win,
yours to be lost and won, and lost and won.

Socrates and the Locusts

Walking up the lawn, I see you through the window
in the room where you are singing—
                              I cannot hear you

through the stolid glass and the blare
of cicadas rising like a sail and as sharp
                              as the needle

that mended the sail in summer heat
where two Greeks lay back in the soft grass,
                              one in his way

teasing the other into truth, or helping him
remember it, since, to the point, all we can do
                  is recollect what we have known

before the beginning of this life in another,
where the men and women who first heard singing
                              could do nothing else

but listen, forgetting to work and play,
love and eat, until they thinned and dried out
                              and became locusts

rattling in their husks, shedding them
in due season, in due season their own rasp
                              only a mocking

of the Muses' first songs—oh, not us,
Socrates chides his friend, we will not give over
                                to the afternoon,

but understand, instead, how lover
and beloved are ladders leading beyond themselves:
                                when the piano strikes

its lovely hammers and character gives birth
to character—Mimi and Suzannah and all the rest
                                who live and die

for love and make a song of it—you make a kind
of love to each, a calculus of passion
                                deeply felt,

and orchestrate the love they make to one another.
But when the music stops, your love stops, too,
                                or dying falls,

or dissipates into the humid air that has received
your song as an offering but muffles now
                                the dissonance of cars

that clack like violent chariots on the road below,
one horse always a little ahead of the other,
                                eyes on the prize

or the whip or the threatening froth about the mouth that stands
for everything—love and purpose and, yes, control,
                              which you do have and do not.

If the Light Could Kill Us

Today has the shimmer of a teen movie.
Our plum tree abundantly pummels
brick by brick the neighbors' pseudo
neoclassical garden. That tree is
oblivious to order. So are the alyssum
and verbena bushes, ablaze with bees.
You are still sleeping, flame-pink
welts our love leaves on your almost
too delicate skin, brazen in this light.
Samuel Johnson is dead. And Mrs. Thrale.
And the kind cherub of a straitjacket
she kept closeted should reason fail
him thoroughly, where's that deck-coat now?
Toothed to dust? A collector's trunk?
Looped around two punks in a London mews
tugging in the dark? On the ship of reason
what's a mutiny? I heard, last night,
our neighbors squabbling over love,
heard the man leave their house and gun
his jeep around the block for hours—
a contagion of chaos. Night's own
stand against us. This morning, violence
lingers like the last touch of a season,
a trail of colored wrappers teenagers leave,
low-riding to road parties at the city's edge.
Only as I rise to pull the window's shade,
do you wake, dusted and dazed, as from a fever.

Toward an Epithalamion

I saw you this morning, early,
      placing flowers
on settlers' graves, the sunken graves
      behind the summer house,
one man's stone, I know,
      an open book—

a wish that we might read him
      from his dust.
Strabo said the world's a coat,
      and if that's right,
it must fall little by little
      from the sky

to cover such cold rests. Think
      of summer clouds
growing full of themselves
      and winnowing
down in shadows instead of rain.
      Two of them

this morning made one shadow
      and gathered us
into its dark cloth, not black
      but a richer green,
a color you've said you'd want
      woven into

a wedding dress or wedding tent.
    I called your name
from the hill, too far away
    for you to hear,
your scarf one tip, my hat the other,
    of our own heraldic shield—

such a stitchery to temper distance.
    It doesn't always
plot against us, this hard earth,
    this solid and
dividing thing. If we marry
    I'll wear the world.

★

I Am Holding a Duckling I Won at the Fair

I am holding a duckling. I am nine years old and wearing my favorite green velour shirt. I am very happy because I won the duckling at the State Fair. At the coin toss booth. I threw my nickel into an empty pie pan and it did not slide out. From a certain angle the duck looks like a rabbit—one of those optical illusions, you know—but it is yellow, so you know it's a duck, and we had rabbits already. We had to kill a black one because my brother left it in a wheelbarrow and it went mad from the summer sun. The duck would grow up. We would give it away. We kept the other rabbits. They lived at night in a hutch next to the raspberry bushes to the left of the clothesline in front of the ashpit that burned in the afternoon and lofted ashes like hopes high into the air and was blanketed on the alley side with mounds and mounds and mounds of emerald green mint.

If Someone Gave Me an Earring

Three nuns sat near the front of the bus—one of them laughed. If I think of the daughter, I thought, I must remember the mother. There are never any real equations. It's difficult to say on what occasions I have died. I can find humiliation in the most everyday things. I have been rewarded by too many people for nothing. I have been ignored by too many for everything. If someone gave me an earring, on which thumb would I wear it? There are so many causes, I have decided not to become one. Can I be absolutely sure but show no outward sign?

I Feel Guilty Watching You Sleep

I feel guilty about watching you sleep because I don't want to wake you. You might attack. It's funny, you know? It's not very good. Maybe it's the garnet on your finger—so many people have tried to steal it. You're incredibly beautiful, tossing and turning when you're asleep. Why do you squint your eyes? And when you pull your hair, why do you pull it? My brother when he was a child used to twirl his hair with one hand and suck the thumb of his other hand. I remember him doing this in front of the china cabinet where there was a porcelain pig that held toothpicks. I was always disappointed that we had light wood cabinets. Because dark wood is more important. I feel so small right now that I wish you'd say "bad" seven times. So I could watch you. I was and still am an altar boy. In a way, that is. We'd get out of school for funerals. I have a poem about being an altar boy at a funeral. The title is a word I made up. I want to know, why does water dry you out? I want to watch you, asleep. The way you sleep when you move your legs is incredible. Did I tell you about the time I saw a woman get hit by a train? It was because the road was wet and her car slid, and this involuntary scream came out of my mouth. It was tangible. I don't know where it came from. When I look at your mouth I am frightened. I'm afraid of what would happen if I woke you up.

I Can't Predict What I Think, I Said

I can't predict what I think, I said with my boots on the desk. But when I was young and we'd drive through the snow, there'd be these pockets of beauty or stillness or something. Where people had been before. It was something I'd look for. We had a pink station wagon. It was lovely. It was going backwards. The machinery was going backwards, but then there was a snap. I lived though. Obviously. My grandfather wasn't there. He had a blue and white Corvair and on the dashboard a pack of Parliament cigarettes which my mother smoked. He used to drive around all night and weep.

Shim Sat and Shat on the Blue Tile Floor

Shim sat and shat on the blue tile floor. He did not squat and he did not think once of his trousers. For fifteen minutes he did not sneeze. "I have never been so *happy*" was one thought he thought. "I have *never* been so happy" was another. He had not just lost his wife. He had not just lost his girlfriend. He was not really looking for this blue tile floor, but there it was. For once, without sneezing, he knew what he wanted. He was not going to weep, he was not going to pray, he was not going to call anyone, collect or otherwise, on the toilet's pay phone. He would shit and he would stand and he would bend to tie his right boot the way he wanted. He would adjust himself. Just the way he wanted. He would start his life again. He would start his life all over again.

Those Years

Friends told you you looked thin,
and they were right, of course.
You had put your life under siege,
half brother of house arrest.
And you tried to explain all this,
though they looked at you as if you'd said
it all began, as it did begin
(not its cause but its *terminus a quo*)
when you saw a dwarf wherever you went,
or a group of them. Even visiting
a friend in the hospital: the elevator
opened and three dwarves got out.

It wasn't, you decided, funny anymore.
Driving up Scotland's east coast yesterday,
it was difficult to believe how hard
you'd been on yourself. What did you gain?
You had your reasons, but now you're for
forgetting them. Just say you resembled
this island—one island and within it
different countries fighting: when Scotland
refused to give their Mary to Henry VIII
to give to his son Edward in marriage,
he sent troops to torch everything they could.
He called it his "rough wooing."

Above St. Andrews, above the cathedral ruins,
someone is popping golf balls into that water trap,
the North Sea. That's silly. Parachutes,
parachutists rather, are falling from a plane
so high you can't see if it's English
or Scottish, its maneuvers filling the morning sky
with white blossoms. They're like memory,
these troopers, disappearing into the waves
only to reappear, later, on the shore.
They're like years you don't exactly want
to remember but want to have back, those years,
and you there to greet them, not like the children

dropping to the sand, pointing their index fingers and shooting,
but the ones scrambling down off the sea wall
and racing toward the soldiers, open-armed and jubilant.

Hospital Corner

Rain's falling on the fifteenth century
and on the courtyard of the Hotel Dieu,
on me as I wonder if it's falling on you
in the semitropical night how many miles away.

Beds line this chapel like a sleeper car,
each bed, curtain opened, has its view
of the altar, its own curtain opened.
Forget the pustules, forget all the lice—

two died to a bed trying to keep warm.
Forget the blunt instruments of surgery—
red blankets and rough, white sheets fold
and tuck tight in the name of charity.

I think of my bed when I was five and sweating
and afraid of circles like sprinkler heads
floating over my fevered hair and face:
in the morning my mother sat me in a chair,

stripped the bed, in slow motion flapped
one clean sheet over her head where
it held a moment, then fell like rain.
How much we can do, how much we cannot do—

the top sheet tucked, sleight of hand,
up, down, triangular, a "hospital corner,"
the clean bed, smoothed, a new birth.
I've wanted to say I have touched too much

mortality for someone as innocent as you.
Rain's falling on the roof of the Hotel Dieu,
and I've wobbled away the tastings of twenty wines
from a *cave* and its bottles across the street.

Twelve French crones, sightseers, too, bundle deep
in a walkway from the courtyard to the gate.
From Beaune to Mexico is almost half the earth.
The house you live in undulates with lice.

Fearless for a public's health, wise, you learn
how much we cannot do and how much we can.
The crones lock hands like children, two by two.
Rain's falling on the gates of the Hotel Dieu.

On the Welsh Coast: Homage to James Joyce

From my window I can almost see
Dublin's watery lamps blink and come on
one by one by one.
I light an orange Welsh candle for

your blurry eyes Ezra Pound called pathological,
and another for your diminutive shoes
and mismatched suits.

Wealth is a shorebird fending for itself,
a tenor voice soothing a salon.
Heat-dried cattails dance
outside in the dusk,

a little family circle. How each of us
bears in the self a trinity of song:
one for the river run of the blood,

one for the long road in
to peat bogs smoldering near a cave
and one for the road back out again.
Summer is a scant week

into itself, and already the bulky ferrymen
have given up on the season: dry-docked,
strike-docked, their boats don't carry

anyone to Dublin. On the boardwalk
in Aberystwyth, tourists stuck in Wales
lament their fortune, tell
again their ill luck. I am reading how

Vikings made the River Liffey move
out of itself and turn closer to the town,
a wall to stop *other* raiders,

a lively vein. It is a sluice, really,
to carry out to sea all sloughed off,
broken, tattered things: lovers' balloons,
widows' weeds. The Irish Sea floor must

be covered with these, each
with a long blue history of its own.
If a small boy chucks a satchel from a bridge

to watch it sink, some afternoon
rain, you can be sure, always, will rain it back again.

For Charles and Mary Lamb

Tonight another room above the Strand,
another Indian restaurant
three doors down. We deal rummy hands
    and brace ourselves
against migratory flights of curries
       clouding the room.

Shuffling the deck, a friend's in no hurry
    to let the cards do
anything but what we say they're meant to—
      draw us into talk
and the innocent vanities and the jests
    Charles delighted in,
sitting, with Mary and friends, at whist.

    Today we walked
past the brownstone we guessed
    Mary killed their mother in.

★

Down Oxford Street and right at Charing Cross,
    past the Strand Hotel and across,

through a Sunday-quiet, tube-entrance tunnel—
    I saw two thousand runners funnel,

this afternoon, onto a road beside the Thames,
    climb the bridge and head back again,

a colorful clot of leaves pushing upriver.
    The marathoners

all had their tested and guessed-at devices
    to pass the point the wall was

likely to hold them at or finish them off.
    It must have been enough,

a way for Charles to push past self-pity,
    to keep living in this city—

how pleased he was with the house he cinched
    a deal for, "forty-two inches

nearer town" than the house before.
    The marathon almost over,

I leave for home across Trafalgar Square,
    punkers with purple hair

flocking around the statue's base like pigeons.
    Black-leathered, legion,

they feign madness as tourists, nervous, laugh
    and pay them to pose for photographs.

★

Last night, down the hall, a cough
    woke me and seemed
my brother's cough, the winter croup
    he often had that enough
vaporizers packed the room we shared,
    puffing out steam
like dead Greeks, their souls seeking air.

    Some nights my mother stooped
to her knees and held him over scalding water
    half-filling the tub.
With her free hand she tried to rub
    his tight muscles loose,
a relative comfort, delicate compared
    to the forgetfulness
we found him, older, face down in,
    bathwater flooding the blue-tiled floor.

We walked him half the night, so shaken
    he didn't say a word.
He slept two days from the pills he'd taken.

★

    How many liberties
we take with others' lives, stories,

   their stories, we tell,
ones they wouldn't tell! How long until

   we let imagination
skew the story line for its own

   sake, or decorum's—
like Charles writing of Mary as his cousin,

   Bridget, forgetting a while
the trips to Hoxton to the private hospital,

   Mary with her wrap,
overnight clothes and her own straitjacket.

   Such recompense
in a change of name, a deuce, for instance,

   becoming different things,
dubbed wild and knighted Jack, crowned Queen.

   Don't call a spade
a spade, call it a heart. Think of, make

   the "shorn Lambs" less
like two: call them a "double singleness."

★

Shoulders bent above his long worktable
	my brother let
blue and yellow watercolors wash
	across paper. Frost
on his window settled in for another night
	he'd worry the house,
asleep while he tossed
	and turned, went back to his desk lamp.

The summer we kept rabbits we left one out
	in the sun one day,
trapped in a wheelbarrow.
	My brother found it in the afternoon,

its eyes and foamy mouth a sorrow
	we didn't know we could have known.

We killed it and put it out of sight—
	as if you could chase
anything away, or make it dear if you tried.

	The last time I went home,
my brother's paintings still hung on the walls,
	memento mori, you could say.
One of the last times I saw him it was fall,
	just before dawn,
sleeping at his desk, a wash not even dry.
	I should have let him stay.

★

A "cow and rabbit couchant, and coextensive,"
   in a "world before perspective"—

Lamb's china teacups: Mandarin women step
   onto light-blue, fairy boats

from a field at least three furlongs off,
   one cherry blossom drops

from mountain to city, a courtly girl hands tea
   across a river garden. She

has as little truck with distance as memory does,
   her black and gold kimono's

hem falling onto both sides of the water
   as if to gather

one hour and the next into a single fold,
   all the young and old

"horses, trees, pagodas, dancing the hays"
   in the lucid air of Cathay.

Can the present finally lie down with the past
   in such an antic peace?

★

I was raised, I remind myself, on emergencies:
    at a siren's high hound
cry my mother warmed the car
   and bundled me in.
With her instinct for near-casualties,
    a bat's sonar
zeroing down, she almost always found
   what she was looking for—
a circle of red lights, a circle of stains.
    Some nights,
up late, I've tried to make it a game
   to guess each siren's goal,
though I'm embarrassed by my need to name
    those children who roll
their parents' cars, or drunks whose wives
   know nothing yet of the half-lives
seeping out and melting the snow.

    It wasn't verity
but near truths that Lamb aimed at,
   not facts but "shadows of facts,"
the half-lies bringing us closer to each other.
    Charles, Mary, please
help me leave the dead to their white privacies.

Tonight Mars Is over by the Moon, Look

Since we've had a brief intermission, Ladies and Gentlemen,
we can be ourselves. I have two pieces of advice:
take everything with you and leave everything behind.
I know I'm not, ultimately, what you asked for,
what you wanted. I was for a while, but yesterday, on the bus
a man said, "I didn't do it. I didn't do anything." And "anything"
remains the word in question, the word operative. For fun, just, I replied,
"Yes, you did." And he laughed. And I did. And I was happy. And the geese,
    now,
flood the lake—"We're halfway between here and there," they say,
so boisterous, so full of their own squawk. A gray cat dances
outside down the street, and tonight the very intimate raccoon has nothing
but good to say. "Why don't you do it?" he whispers. "Why don't
you put on your shoes and be who you are—whoever *that* might be?"
I couldn't reply. At all. The raccoon shuddered. And two or three
of his friends joined up with him. They stared at me. They seemed to buddy
    up.
Then they slipped down the storm drain with hardly, barely, a sound.

There, That's It

For Lynne B., off to thirty days in the Summit County Jail

When the bell rings I hear your name.
The obsidian on the playground wears through my sneakers,
even though we are just playing. Today, again on the bus,
I saw a twenty-five-year-old sucking his thumb.
That was not secure. There is a road in southern Colorado
that is. Secure, that is. When the lights go out,
I'll see you equine. Your face. And full of heart.
There is that road there that you can smell and taste.
I will show it to you. I am a child. I love you.
There is a tree, too, in southern Colorado that grows close to the ground,
and say, let's just say, they're three feet off, the limbs that move out and out.
And where do they go? Nobody knows. You can smell that tree, taste it.
It never ends. It. I would do anything for you. But you know that.
When the bell rings, school is in, and yes, also, school is out. Ever.

Chanteuse with Dog, Walking

They are public. They do not keep to themselves.
If you listen you can just hear the dog singing.
The park today, the park buzzes with bicycles,
each of them a song: red and blue and so metallic,
couples on two-seaters, ghetto bikes without color,
bicycles with playing cards festooned to their spokes—
ace, fwap, deuce, fwap, faster fwapapapapapap.

All the men's hats go up and up and down.
So many hats for the lateness of our own time!
Women look her in the eye. She looks them in the eye,
and she is pleased. They are pleased. But no one
is more pleased than the chanteuse's sleek spaniel.

A song for a king's death, a song for a bum's life,
and for the soldiers, their legs crooked in the night.
For a queen's coronation, her nation's sweet nipple.
The spaniel is proud to be at this end of this leash.
He's seen the down on her arms and been rightly humble,
and waited in the window, her clickclick up the sidewalk.
She's known what it is to sing all a beast's sorrows.

Three for One

For MT, assaulted at ten

This Has Nothing to Do With Me

"Someone has been killing me in my sleep.
Either that or I'm suffering from nothing less than the loss of music
and the green barrette I wore in my hair when I was ten.
If I had known how to say it I would have said
     'Put down that fucking broom—you're sweeping me off my feet.'
It is, however, the only springtime I remember:
    I chopped off my hair,
    I beat up a boy in the park,
    I wore a green barrette in the farthest corner of my mind."

My Black Cat Dances to Gounod's "Ave Maria"

"I told you I wasn't flirting with the police—I was only five.
I must have been showing them the mountain lion
    my grandfather shot.
Whenever I find something the color of ticking, I want to hold it.
So what if the family car cuts circles on the front lawn—
my mother was driving, my daddy hung on to the hood.
My grandmother emptied our house of all of its furniture,
    stick by stick, all by herself.

The ambush began each afternoon as I sat down at the piano
    and started to play.
Hey Borodin! Hey Chopin! Hey . . . you . . . Romeo!
Let's see, did I have one blister on my trigger finger, or two?
I'll tell you what: I've forgotten to care."

Sal DeRose Taught Me How to Swim. Who Taught You?

"I used to ride on the hood of dad's jeep when he hunted for birds.
I used to canoe in the pond just over that hill.
Remember carrying me on your shoulders at night
    in my mother's pool, and I was naked?
I knew it would kill you, I knew you would dream of me
    all night long.
I want you between my legs, I want your hands on my temples.

Okay, so it's Christmas. So my sister's sedated.
We sit on the veranda snapping twigs off trees with our rifles.
I know that we scare you. I know I might love you.
I want to take you to a baseball game, not here but in the
    mountains,
where the stars sing 'Batter, batter, batter,'
    and the blue moon calls out 'Batter up!'"

Contrecoup

Also for MT

Yes, the cotton ball *can* be used in many ways: blocking noise
and the freezing wind and stoppering the slick blood
slipping from your nose, and taking off, when you wear makeup, your face.
It is not much good with tears, unless they are few.
Sure, you can soothe the spider bite with a little alcohol,
and just maybe you can get out all of the poison,
but you're right as right it's still going to leave a dent,
one dent, strangely attractive. That's cause and effect, the dent,
isn't it? Which sometimes I understand, sometimes I don't.
Especially when it's this because of that because of that. . . .

Oh, how our brains float in our skulls like a saline breast!
A shar-pei bouncing, as they say, off the walls of the obscure room.
Say you hit your head hard enough, or someone hits it for you,
hard enough—it's not the first hit, but the ricochet, the contrecoup,
that will do it. The dent inside, on the other side now. You know,
the other blow the green-gowned doctor said absolutely floored you.

This Is the Library Straight down from the Train Room

This library is for children, and the train room is, too.
We had a train room in our house when I was nine.
My brother built it. It was sort of square.
But it was in the basement, and it opened onto a bigger room—
you could close it off, though, with one of those bamboo curtains,
you know? My brother made it, the train room. Why, yes he did.
He knew how to make things, my brother. He could make trains,
and—you know what?—he could make bridges and towns, too.

And I put people in them. And yellow lights late at night,
and gravel and green grass during the day, and families and filling stations
and switching stations and train cars that were chock-full of stories
about madness and jubilance. You might break your heart, you know,
    having a train room.

You might learn how to live—how things are, the way stories are, made.

Processionalia

Out the shaganappy of Colorado Highway 50,
        past Damon Runyon
    Stadium and the steel-mill lake,
slag-pocket, second home for petulant
        boozers, past
    the Greenwood Inn's music
still playing into morning for fourteen-
        year-old boy-men
    slow dancing with divorcees,
past fields of radishes and Italian farmers
        as thick as Chevys, past pink,
    purple, robin's-
egg-blue slick coats of Mexican shacks
        and the goat-cheese shop,
    its parking lot
full of black cars rumored bigwig Mafiosi's,
        past the wrought-iron gates
    and heavenly angels
guarding Roselawn Cemetery with marble
        swords, past the blue-jeaned
    groundskeepers joking
as they put away their shovels, past
        all this scholia
    to the canopied gathering
and my ten-year-old, acolyte, altar-boy self
        giving up cub-reporter
    daydreams, home-run daydreams,

but not looking at the bronze casket he'll
              get ten bucks for
       helping lower and not looking either
   at the protandric priest's smooth-shaven jowls
              or the blanket of flowers
       rising from the lawn like phosphorescent
   anger, but watching, instead, a bee
              abandon the tea roses
       and circle that black blossom of
   the widow's veiled face as if her tears were
       pollen and the bee could feather
              its legs with grief
   and change it—can grief ever change?—into honey.

The Rainbow Diary

It's summertime. Let's go everybody. Everybody ready?
A family packing for a trip, three boys, their hair cut
in burrs, the mother holding a camp stool and looking
at the oldest boy who's looking at the middle boy who's
looking at the youngest while they duel with fishing rods
and the father looks at the mother. Will they catch many fish?
How much will be spoken? How much will be left unspoken?
See the youngest slit his thigh with the fish knife? Watch
the middle boy, his hand severed by the outboard and drifting
like a small shoe toward the lake bottom. Is the oldest losing
an eye, the iris snagged like a rainbow trout? Is the father
driving their car, with all of them in it, into the river?
Is the mother whispering prayers? How much love can they kill?
How many fish can they catch? How many will they throw back?
How many will get away? See the car fly backward from river
to road? Such a home movie! Watch the boy's hand turn and swim
back to its wrist and join—how the skin sutures itself!
They're teasing over dinner. No furies, no sudden danger.
What about hope? What about the blue and yellow and orange
pages of the mother's journal? "Today, dear diary, another first...."

Christmas, Colorado

The nun's gray robes are a clue
to the girl whose darkening lungs
we pray for at school.
That we imagine those lungs were once white as milk
but are gathering black spots like flies
seems only natural.
We have learned that the white fist
of the soul remains clean
a short while. Then it, too, dabs itself
with bruises.

But in Christmas, Colorado, we are glad
you can find our town on a calendar
as well as a map,
on the Advent wreath with its pink and violet candles
we light each week moving toward Christmas.
Later we will learn
how small we are, a pinprick in location
and time. For now, there is sadness
only in the name we say again and again
in our parade of prayers.

A one-way street or a circle?
She'll be there again in the words whispered over
    our beds,
"Jenny, you don't have to pray for Jenny anymore."
Sparkle amber, sparkle scarlet, sparkle green.

She is the strip of light under the bedroom door,
a blanket of December snow.

All Hallows Eve / Anniversary

I

The room is halved this late afternoon
by a pale-orange sun,

your drying rack and French peasant soap
crowding your corner, your coat

spread out on wood rungs to dry,
a ghost of your body. You will arrive,

return, in an hour or so. On the table,
a drawing pad, a drawing of a turtle—

how strongly, when you're out, I feel you here.
This will be our fourth year.

II

Already by dusk, children of the poor
gather on street corners

in Pueblo, Colorado. A pickup truck
glides through its litany

of streets, dropping newspaper bundles
like stones. The children light stump candles

and move in gold procession to the church.
Saints listen into the river, in their turn,

dying again, each evening, equivocal,
all their modesties tested by soft vowels.

III

All Hallows Eve—my sixth,
costumed and candid, a John the Baptist

in burlap coat and charcoal beard
like other children's hobos but scared

of the prophet's headless fate,
a reed in the desert, one that breaks

sharply in the wind—the dried stems
of fraxinella neighbors pinned

onto porch poles. Those buds in June,
their heavy vapors, could burst into flame.

IV

The candles we placed on the porch this year
are burning slowly, no wind to blur

their almond eyes. They'll melt down
in their sweet time, all four fingers gone

into a mitten of warm wax.
We'll touch our hands together to the glass

for another year's luck, as groups of children
in their costumes wobble up our walk—

tigers, angels, the turtle with its shell,
simple and steadfast and durable.

Summer Indians

I

The Gallup, New Mexico, Festival of Indian Dances
lasted one week each July, a round of gods
and coyotes, mudmen and Koshare clowns. Innocent,
I found it pure ritual, not staged or happenstance:
the dancers had the power to draw a dozen clouds
out of the clear, thin air to rain on their dry crops,
and they were kind to me, a child lost in their midst
a whole half-day while my parents searched the crowd.
Indians fed me stew and corn, forgiving me the scent
of my white flesh and set a blanket on the ground.
I could not rest. I watched as they brought back
a young, boozy man—firewater—from a bus-stop bench
and laid him in the shade and dabbed his face. "An Indian
in New Mexico," a tourist said, "is a Mexican's Mexican."

II

Bohunk, greaseball, jungle bunny, mick,
beaner, coconut, mau mau, Polack, spic—
epithets rising like cheers from a football game.
Too young to leave my seat I heard rumbles at the gate
and the horseshoe curves of the football stands
at half-time intermission. Tight, hungry bands

ignored the one marching on the field and played
their interlude with brass knuckles and switchblades,
and baseball bats when the fight was close to lost.
Their fathers waited afterward in bars across
from the steel-mill stacks, coal cars and the slag,
each bar a little country with its own bright flag.
They set up shots for fights they would not stop.
By day they worked together in the slag mill's melting pot.

III

Our parents must have thought us odd redactors,
their Colorado interest in the history of the West:
our living room, circa 1960, pre-shag wood floors,
green drapes with greener swirls, built-in cabinets,
a circular, purposeless railing near the clock
where we'd later build a staircase to the cellar,
the circle serving for our Indian tribal fires
around which we would whoop and scream and double up
with perfect savage grace, dressed and wrought
to kill, if in pretend—bear-claw necklaces and bows,
beaded leather leggings, bracelets, armbands, arrows,
headdresses tiaraed with pigeon feathers, not hawk—
attempts like our own to be something they were not,
ranch-housed as we were, country-clubbed and white.

IV

Mike Sweeney, Spencer Tillman, Tony Amayo,
in black and white and brown and letter sweaters, the halls
of high school a paean to football, baseball, basketball
and the legends of less organized peccadilloes:
Mike crossing the Eighth Street Bridge to the West Side
only to be chased back with rocks and two-by-fours
laced with three-penny nails; the night the doors
of Spencer Tillman's house were upholstered with raccoon hides;
the day lovesick Tony gave a white girl looks,
her brothers found him, pinned him and broke his hands.
Red scalps white and white scalps red in the Sand
Creek Massacre, says my childhood, hardback Indian book.
I turn pages to find Cochise, Custer, Geronimo
in daguerreotype on the eves of their last stands.

V

I wonder what he's doing now, Thomas Hope,
the only black kid in my heatstoked, crowded room
in Pueblo, Colorado, in a West Side barrio school—
the way he laughed when I stopped him as he loped
across the playground, to ask what his mother cooked
that clung to his check shirt, his little jeans and his jacket
and smelled so good. "My daddy cooked a jackrabbit,"

he told me and ran off to play a dark Captain Hook
to his Chicano friends' Peter Pan and Tinker Bell,
a story so lily-white I didn't think they'd know
or care about Wendy and Michael and John. "I gotta crow—
cock-a-doodle-doo," their voices, Thomas's voice, swelled,
as they shed narrative and role, praise and blame,
to wake the world to the sweet gift of his last name.

★

Blue

Blue was the color of my shirt the day I grew up.
    I haven't seen that shade since.

I remember looking over at my father,
    staring at him until his face turned to bone and bliss.

I saw that he was red around the neck,
    but I was wrong.

His color was blue, just like mine.

I walked over to pick him up, and all the stories he had always told me
    fell out of his pockets.

I turned off the music and refused to hear them,

took the gun out of my book bag
    and shot my breakfast.

    ★

I was looking down the stairs at my brother.
    He looked like nothing or no one I had ever seen before.

There was something strange about him: the shoulder pads,
    I don't know, the numbers on his chest.

He took a violin off the shelf and started to play
    "Blue Danube" or maybe another song I'd heard before.

I can't remember.

I do remember sitting at the top of the stairs,
    looking at the animal in the doorway—

it had my brother's feet, and I wanted to run,
    and I wanted to sit there for a very long time.

    ★

I found a blue slip that once belonged to my mother.
    It smelled like mint.

I thought at first it belonged to someone I didn't know,
    but I was wrong. Again.

My dad had a cobalt blue glass.
    My mother had a slip with a cigarette burn in it—

I packed my father's glass and my mother's slip in a suitcase
    and buried it underneath the very big tree.

That was the last time I saw my two brothers.
    My one brother, I'm sorry, I mean. I only had one.

    ★

I borrowed a box car from the county zoo.
    No, I didn't. That was a dream.

I started the car out in the famous two-car garage—
    I always dreamed of driving fast.

I put the key in the ignition like a big boy would,

then I hesitated, because that was my nature—
    to stop once before I went in for the kill.

But when I saw the blue smoke I remembered loving me
    wouldn't be what I expected.

It's never what I expect.
    And starting cars makes me feel dead.

★

I remember seeing my first blue moon
    on the highway going north.

I was in a stolen car. I was famous.
    I *felt* famous.

Like everyone was watching me:
    there was blue snow, with trillions of eyes

and the memory of two people bound and gagged in the trunk,
   but I can't remember if they were men or women.

I can't remember if one or both were drunk,
   but I remember liking a pair of cowboy boots.

Guess what color they were.

★

It's ten till the witching hour. Make that eleven.
   Wrong again.

My brother is holding a gun on me, I think,
   and I can't even hear the record player.

Just the dull dirge coming off the radiator.
   Or "Blue Danube" or "Blue Velvet."

Come over here, and I'll smile for you, he says.
   And I love my brother, so I do.

He touches my hand and tells me
   never to think such a blue blue blue....

★

My brother tried to love me once.
    My father took a picture of it from the doorway.

My mother lay in our bed with her favorite slip on.
    My mother lay in our bed smoking a cigarette.

I tried to tell her good night,
    but she had her hand over my mouth by then,

and I was biting it or licking or kissing it.
    I was around nine or ten.

I have a blue car now. I call it Colorado,
    not Montana or Coeur D'Alene.

Colorado is where I lived once, where I grew up,
    every time I remember that name.

Martin McGovern earned his MA in philosophy at Stanford University and his PhD in creative writing/literature at the University of Houston's Creative Writing Program. His poetry, essays, and reviews have appeared in *The New Republic, Poetry, Denver Quarterly, Hotel Amerika, Chicago Review, Kenyon Review, Sewanee Review,* and elsewhere. He cofounded  The Urban Theater Company in Houston and was Associate Artistic Director of Ad Hoc Theater and Artistic Director of Tir Na nOg: An Irish Theater in Denver. His play "Joseph K" earned the 2009 Denver Post Ovation Award for Best New Work. Having taught for Regis University's College for Professional Studies since 2007 and creating its MA in Creative Writing, McGovern is also now cofounder and codirector of that university's Mile-High Low-Residency MFA program.

Also from Able Muse Press

William Baer, *Times Square and Other Stories*
Melissa Balmain, *Walking in on People – Poems*
Ben Berman, *Strange Borderlands – Poems*
Michael Cantor, *Life in the Second Circle – Poems*
Catherine Chandler, *Lines of Flight – Poems*
William Conelly, *Uncontested Grounds – Poems*
Maryann Corbett, *Credo for the Checkout Line in Winter – Poems*
John Drury, *Sea Level Rising – Poems*
D.R. Goodman, *Greed: A Confession – Poems*
Margaret Ann Griffiths, *Grasshopper – The Poetry of M A Griffiths*
Ellen Kaufman, *House Music – Poems*
Carol Light, *Heaven from Steam – Poems*
April Lindner, *This Bed Our Bodies Shaped – Poems*
Jeredith Merrin, *Cup – Poems*
Richard Newman, *All the Wasted Beauty of the World – Poems*
Frank Osen, *Virtue, Big as Sin – Poems*
Alexander Pepple (Editor), *Able Muse Anthology*
Alexander Pepple (Editor), *Able Muse – a review of poetry, prose & art* (semiannual issues, Winter 2010 onward)
James Pollock, *Sailing to Babylon – Poems*
Aaron Poochigian, *The Cosmic Purr – Poems*
Stephen Scaer, *Pumpkin Chucking – Poems*
Hollis Seamon, *Corporeality – Stories*
Matthew Buckley Smith, *Dirge for an Imaginary World – Poems*
Barbara Ellen Sorensen, *Compositions of the Dead Playing Flutes – Poems*
Wendy Videlock, *The Dark Gnu and Other Poems*
Wendy Videlock, *Nevertheless – Poems*
Wendy Videlock, *Slingshots and Love Plums – Poems*
Richard Wakefield, *A Vertical Mile – Poems*
Chelsea Woodard, *Vellum – Poems*

www.ablemusepress.com

www.ingramcontent.com/pod-product-compliance
Lightning Source LLC
Chambersburg PA
CBHW031607110426
42742CB00037B/1322